# Maine

by Patricia K. Kummer,
the Capstone Press Geography Department

**Content Consultant:**
Connie Manter
Maine Department of Education

CAPSTONE PRESS
MANKATO, MINNESOTA

C A P S T O N E    P R E S S

818 North Willow Street • Mankato, MN 56001

http://www.capstone-press.com

Printed in the United States of America.

*Library of Congress Cataloging-in-Publication Data*
Kummer, Patricia K.
   Maine/by Patricia K. Kummer.
   p. cm.--(One nation)
   Includes bibliographical references and index.
   Summary: An overview of the history, geography, people, and living conditions of the state of Maine.
   ISBN 1-56065-526-7
   1. Maine--Juvenile literature. [1. Maine.]
   I. Title. II. Series.
F19.3.K86 1998
974.1--dc21

                              97-6328
                               CIP
                               AC

Photo credits
Archive Photos, 25
Capstone Press, 4 (left)
Peter Ford, 8, 10, 22, 26, 33
International Stock/Mimi Cotter, 20
G. Alan Nelson, cover, 34
Penobscot Indian Reservation/Community Building, 18
Richard Procopio, 5 (left and right), 6, 12, 16, 29, 30
Root Resources/Alan Nelson, 4 (right)

# Table of Contents

# Fast Facts about Maine

**State Flag**

**Location**: In the New England region of the northeastern United States

**Size**: 35,387 square miles (92,006 square kilometers)

**Population**: 1,241,382 (1995 United States Census Bureau figures)

**Capital**: Augusta

**Date admitted to the Union**: March 15, 1820; the 23rd state

**Chickadee**

**White pine cone and tassel**

**Largest cities**: Portland, Lewiston, Bangor, Auburn, South Portland, Augusta, Biddeford, Waterville, Westbrook, Saco

**Nickname**: The Pine Tree State
**State animal**: Moose
**State bird**: Chickadee
**State flower**: White pine cone and tassel
**State tree**: White pine
**State song**: "State of Maine Song" by Roger Vinton Snow

**White pine**

# *Chapter 1*

# Maine's Lighthouses

More than 60 lighthouses line the Maine coast. Whaleback Lighthouse is the farthest south. It stands at Kittery. West Quoddy Head Lighthouse is the farthest north. It stands at Lubec.

Most of Maine's lighthouses are still operating. They shine bright lights over the sea. The lights warn ships not to come closer. This prevents shipwrecks from happening on Maine's rough and rocky coast.

All of Maine's operating lighthouses are automated. This means their lights are timed to go off and on by themselves. Lighthouse keepers are no longer needed to turn on the lights.

**More than 60 lighthouses line the Maine coast.**

Portland Head Light is Maine's oldest lighthouse. George Washington signed the order to build it.

### Portland Head Light

Portland Head Light is Maine's oldest lighthouse. It is on Cape Elizabeth. President George Washington signed the order to build this lighthouse. It was the first one built by the U.S. government. The light at Portland Head has warned ships of danger since 1791.

The lighthouse keeper's cottage is now a museum. Visitors can learn about the history of lighthouses. The museum's displays also tell about the history of sailing.

## Other Sea Attractions

People catch more lobsters in Maine than in any other state. The state's coastal restaurants serve fresh lobster. Many people believe Maine lobsters taste the best. Lobsters grow large in Maine's cold water.

People from Maine are called Mainers. Many Mainers and visitors enjoy sailing. They take week-long cruises on windjammers. A windjammer is a large ship with two tall sails. Most cruises leave from Rockland or Camden.

Boothbay Harbor celebrates Windjammer Days in July. During the celebration, old schooners sail into the harbor. A schooner is a fast ship with two sails. These ships once carried goods. They took long voyages.

Some Maine visitors learn how to build boats. They attend the Wooden Boat School. This is in Brooklin. In six days, a team builds a cedar boat.

# *Chapter 2*
# **The Land**

Maine is the farthest northeast of all the states. The nation's easternmost point is West Quoddy Head in Maine.

Maine is also the largest of the six New England states. New Hampshire forms Maine's western border.

Two Canadian provinces also border Maine. New Brunswick is to the north and east. Quebec lies to the north and west.

The Atlantic Ocean forms Maine's southern border. This tidal shoreline is 3,478 miles (5,565 kilometers) long. It includes all of Maine's bays, inlets, and islands. Casco and Penobscot are two large bays.

**The Atlantic Ocean forms Maine's southern edge.**

## Coastal Lowlands and the Upland

The Coastal Lowlands lie inland from the Atlantic. There, Maine reaches its lowest point at sea level. Sandy beaches lie along the southern part of the coast. Rugged cliffs stand along the northern part of the coast.

More than 400 islands lie off Maine's shores. Mount Desert Island is the largest one. It is 100 square miles (160 square kilometers) in size.

Maine's upland lies north of the Coastal Lowlands. It covers most of Maine. The upland has many forests and level land.

The Aroostook Plateau stretches across the northeastern upland. It has rich soil. Farmers grow large crops of potatoes and oats there.

## Maine's White Mountains

The White Mountains rise in northwestern Maine. They are part of the Appalachian Mountains.

Mount Katahdin is Maine's highest point. It stands 5,268 feet (1,580 meters) above sea level. That is almost one mile (one and one-half kilometers) high.

Forests cover most of the White Mountains. Melted ice from glaciers formed hundreds of lakes

**Mount Katahdin is Maine's highest point.**

there, too. Glaciers are large sheets of slowly moving ice.

Moosehead Lake is Maine's largest lake. It covers about 120 square miles (312 square kilometers). This lake is shaped like a moose head with antlers.

## Maine's Rivers

Three rivers form Maine's border with Canada. They are the St. Francis, the St. John, and the St. Croix rivers.

More than 5,000 rivers and streams wind through Maine. They empty into the Atlantic Ocean. The Androscoggin, Kennebec, and Penobscot are Maine's longest rivers.

## Forests and Wildlife

Maine is the nation's most wooded state. White pine and Norway pine are its main trees.

Bobcats and black bears live in Maine's mountains. Moose feed along the lakes. Seals play along the coast. Puffins and snowy egrets nest there.

Trout and salmon swim in Maine's lakes and rivers. Lobsters and clams live in coastal waters.

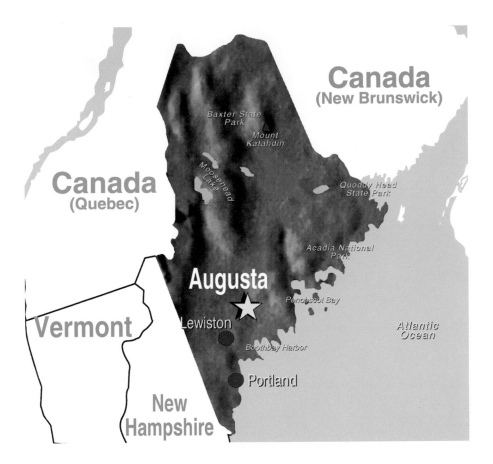

## Climate

Maine's summers are cool. Its winters are cold. In the fall, strong windstorms hit the coast. The storms are called northeasters. They whip up huge ocean waves.

Maine receives a lot of snow each year. The coast receives about five feet (one and one-half meters). The northern mountains can receive more than nine feet (three meters).

# Chapter 3

# The People

Maine is the least crowded eastern state. It has the 13th smallest population among the 50 states.

Few people live in northern and western Maine. It is still wilderness. Most Mainers live close to the coast. About 25 percent live near Portland. This is Maine's largest city.

Maine is still a rural state. About 55 percent of Mainers live far from cities. Some have farms. A few have homes in the mountains or woods. Others live in small fishing villages.

## Maine's Largest Population Group

About 98 percent of Mainers are white. Their families came from Europe, Canada, and the Middle East.

**Northern and western Maine is still wilderness.**

**The Penobscot have the largest reservation in Maine.**

Today, about 60 percent of Mainers have English backgrounds. French Americans make up the next largest group. Other Mainers have Irish, German, Italian, Polish, or Lebanese backgrounds.

## French Americans

More than 110,000 French Americans live in Maine. Some of them have Acadian backgrounds. Acadians are French people who once lived in Nova Scotia, Canada. The British forced them out of Canada in the 1750s. Today, most of Maine's Acadians live along the St. John River.

Other French-speaking people have come from Quebec, Canada. Biddeford and Lewiston have large French Canadian populations.

French is spoken in many Maine homes. The French Americans publish French-language newspapers. Some radio stations broadcast programs in French.

## Native Americans

About 6,000 Native Americans live in Maine today. The Passamaquoddy and Penobscot are the largest groups. Some Micmac and Malecite also live there.

Maine has four reservations. A reservation is land set aside for use by Native Americans. The Penobscot have the largest reservation. It covers 146 islands in the Penobscot River.

The Passamaquoddy have two reservations. They are close to Perry and Calais. The Passamaquoddy host Ceremonial Day near Perry on August 1. Canoe races, singing, and dancing are part of the celebration.

## African Americans

African Americans have lived in Maine since the 1600s. Some came as servants. Others worked as slaves. In 1776, about 500 African Americans lived there.

Slavery ended in Maine in 1783. Many African Americans living in Maine moved closer to cities. Others farmed or fished. By 1860, about 1,300 African Americans lived in Maine. Today, Maine has about 5,000 African Americans.

## Other Ethnic Groups

Maine also has small Hispanic American and Asian American populations. Mexicans and Puerto Ricans are Maine's largest Hispanic groups.

Most of Maine's Asian Americans are Chinese or Filipino. Recently, many Vietnamese and Cambodians have arrived.

**Today, Maine has about 5,000 African Americans.**

# Chapter 4
# Maine History

People first lived in Maine about 10,000 years ago. By the 1400s, several Native American groups lived there. They included the Passamaquoddy and Penobscot.

## English and French Explorers

By 1524, explorers for both England and France had reached Maine. They saw Maine's riches, including forests, animal furs, and fish. Both countries claimed the area.

The French named their land Acadia. This included Canada and Maine. They built forts and trading posts in eastern Maine.

In the 1620s, English settlers came to southwestern Maine. Many of them were from

French and English explorers saw Maine's forests, animal furs, and fish.

Massachusetts. In 1677, Maine became part of the Massachusetts colony. A colony is a group of people who settle in a different land but remain subject to their native country.

## The French and Indian Wars

France and England struggled for control of North America. They fought the French and Indian Wars (1689-1763). Native Americans helped the French.

England won the French and Indian Wars. France lost Acadia. England gained control of all of Maine.

## The Revolutionary War

England had 13 colonies in North America. In 1775, the colonies rebelled against English taxes. They started the Revolutionary War (1775-1783). English troops burned Portland in 1775. Mainers captured an English ship at Machias.

The colonies won the war. They became the United States of America. At that time, Maine was still part of Massachusetts.

## Growth of Maine

From 1790 to 1810, more than 130,000 people settled in the Maine area. Many came from the

**English troops burned Portland during the Revolutionary War in 1775.**

present-day Massachusetts area and New Hampshire.

Maine's lumber business grew. Mainers built ships with the wood. Maine's ships sailed around the world. Trade with other countries became important.

## Maine Becomes a State

The United States and England fought another war over land. This was the War of 1812 (1812-1815). During this war, English troops occupied

eastern Maine. Massachusetts did not protect Maine. The war hurt Maine's trade.

The United States won the war. Mainers asked to separate from Massachusetts. In 1820, Maine became the 23rd state. Portland was the first capital. Augusta became the capital in 1832.

Between 1820 and 1860, Maine's population grew by 300,000. Fishing, shipping, and logging also grew. Granite and limestone mining became important, too.

The ice industry began. Ice was cut from Maine's rivers and lakes. It was shipped to southern cities.

## The Civil War

Slavery divided the nation. Those in the North were against slavery. The South was for slavery. As a Northern state, Maine was against slavery. Mainers worked to end slavery in the South.

Slavery was a major cause of the Civil War (1861-1865). Maine helped the North win that war. More than 73,000 Maine soldiers served in the Northern army. In 1865, the North won the war, and all the slaves were freed.

**Mainers act out Civil War battles. The war divided the nation in the 1860s.**

## New Industries

By the late 1800s, Maine had many railroads. The Aroostook Railroad carried potatoes to market. Potatoes became Maine's leading crop.

Textile and paper mills were built along Maine's rivers. Shoemaking factories were built, too. The Bath Iron Works built steel ships.

## Prohibition, Depression, and World War II

In 1846, Maine passed the nation's first state law making alcoholic drinks illegal. This law was called prohibition. Making and selling alcoholic drinks was illegal in Maine until 1856. In 1919, the United States started Prohibition. This made alcoholic drinks illegal in all the states. Some Mainers sneaked whiskey in from Canada. Prohibition ended in 1933.

The Great Depression (1929-1939) hurt the entire country. Maine's potato prices fell. Factories closed. People lost their jobs.

In 1941, the United States entered World War II (1939-1945). Maine's shipyards built destroyers and cargo ships. Factories made uniforms and boots.

**The Bath Iron Works was a new industry in the late 1800s. Steel ships were built there.**

## Recent Challenges

Clams and cod were dying in Cosco Bay. Mainers wanted to protect their environment from pollution. Mainers started working to clean up the bay.

Clear-cutting of forests worried Mainers, too. Clear-cutting is cutting down whole areas of trees.

In 1996, however, Mainers voted not to ban clear-cutting. They wanted to protect Maine's workers. Logging and paper companies employ many people.

## Chapter 5
# Maine Business

Maine has worked hard to attract new businesses in recent years. The state wanted to bring down its unemployment rate. In 1994, Maine had the nation's fourth highest unemployment rate.

Manufacturing is Maine's most valuable business. Taken together, however, service industries lead Maine's businesses. They include tourism and trade.

## Manufacturing

Paper and forestry are important Maine manufacturing businesses. Paper goods include cardboard boxes, paper bags, and newsprint.

Lumber is Maine's leading wood product. The state leads the nation in making wooden toothpicks.

**Forestry is one of Maine's most important businesses.**

Lobster traps, clothespins, and matches are other wood products made in Maine.

Shipbuilding and boat building are important in southwestern Maine. Electronics companies make parts for computers.

## Service Industries

Tourism is also a very important Maine business. Each year, tourists spend about $2 billion in the state. Many people stay at coastal hotels and visit ski resorts.

Trade is another important service industry. L. L. Bean is one of Maine's most famous stores. It is in Freeport. More than 3 million people shop there each year. L. L. Bean also sells its goods through the mail.

Overseas trade is important, too. Eastport has the nation's closest port to Europe.

## Agriculture

Potatoes are Maine's most valuable crop. The state ranks eighth among the nation's potato producers. Apples and blueberries are important fruit crops.

Southern Maine has many dairy and egg farms. Milk is the leading livestock product.

**Maine leads the nation in catching lobsters.**

## Fishing and Mining

Almost every coastal village has a fishing fleet. Maine leads the nation in catching lobsters. It is second to Maryland in catching clams.

Southwestern Maine has large sand and gravel mines. Limestone is also mined in Maine. Tourmaline, amethyst, and topaz are mined there, too. These are gemstones. They are often used in jewelry.

# Chapter 6

# Seeing the Sights

Maine's coast, woods, and mountains offer outdoor fun. The cities and museums help visitors learn about Maine's history.

## The Southwestern Coast

Kittery is at Maine's southwestern tip. Fort McClary is close to the ocean. It was built in 1690. Soldiers at this fort guarded Maine during five wars.

Kennebunkport is north of Kittery. It has the Seashore Trolley Museum. About 200 streetcars are displayed there. Visitors can ride one of them.

Old Orchard Beach is farther north. This is one of Maine's best sand beaches. It has an

**Moosehead Lake is Maine's largest lake.**

amusement park, too. Visitors can ride a Ferris wheel and look out at the ocean.

Portland is even farther north. It is a great shipping center. Ships from all over the world dock there. Portland has rebuilt its waterfront. It is called the Old Port Exchange. These buildings from the 1870s now have shops and restaurants in them.

## Interior Cities

Lewiston and Auburn are north and inland from Portland. They are called the Twin Cities. The Androscoggin River flows between them.

Augusta is northeast of the Twin Cities. This is the state capital. The capitol building is made of Maine granite.

Bangor is farther northeast. The famous author Stephen King lives there. He writes horror books.

## The Middle Coast

Bath is north of Portland on the middle coast. Bath is a great shipbuilding city. The Maine Maritime Museum is there. Historic wooden ships are docked at the museum.

Hog Island is east of Bath. Young people can attend a camp there. They learn about nature and the environment.

Rockland is on Penobscot Bay. Each August, the town hosts the Maine Lobster Festival.

## The Northeastern Coast

Acadia National Park is east of Penobscot Bay. This is New England's only national park. Most of the park is on Mount Desert Island.

Acadia National Park has lakes and forests. The Atlantic Coast's highest point is in the park. This is Cadillac Mountain. It is 1,530 feet (459 meters) above sea level. Visitors can drive to the top of the mountain.

Eastport is northeast of Acadia National Park. It is the nation's easternmost city. West Quoddy Head is the easternmost point. When the sun rises, Maine is the first of the states to see it.

## Northern Maine

Presque Isle is in northeastern Maine. It is northern Maine's largest city. Presque Isle has a well-known potato market.

The Allagash Wilderness Waterway is in northwestern Maine. It is more than 90 miles (144 kilometers) long. Some people canoe the entire waterway. The trip can take 10 days.

At the end of the waterway is Baxter State Park. The park has 45 mountains. The tallest is Mount Katahdin. It takes a long time to climb to the top.

Patten is east of the park. The Lumberman's Museum is there. It has more than 4,000 displays in 10 buildings. They explain life in Maine's logging camps.

The Forks is southwest of Baxter State Park. Many whitewater rafters set off from there. They take an exciting ride down the Kennebec River.

## Western Lakes and Mountains

Tims Pond is west of The Forks. It is a popular place for catching brook trout. The oldest sports camp in the country is there.

Livermore is south of Tims Pond. Norlands Living History Center is outside the town. Families can stay at the history center for three days. They live as farm families did in 1870.

Bethel is west of Livermore. Many ski resorts are near this town. One resort is Sunday River. It has some of the nation's best downhill skiing. More than 100 trails weave through the mountains.

# Maine Time Line

**10,000 B.C.**—The first people arrive in Maine.

**A.D. 1400s**—The Passamaquoddy, Penobscot, and Kennebec people are living in Maine.

**1497-1499**—John Cabot explores Maine's coast and claims the land for England.

**1524**—Giovanni da Verrazano explores Maine's coast and claims the land for France.

**1623**—Saco becomes Maine's first permanent English settlement.

**1677**—The area now called Maine becomes part of Massachusetts.

**1689-1763**—The French and Native Americans try to gain control of Maine.

**1775**—The first sea battle of the Revolutionary War is fought off Machias.

**1820**—Maine is admitted to the Union as the 23rd state.

**1832**—The capital is moved from Portland to Augusta.

**1842**—The United States and England set Maine's northern boundary at the St. Francis River.

**1870s**—Maine becomes a popular summer resort area.

**1898**—The battleship *Maine* is blown up in Havana, Cuba, which starts the Spanish-American War.

**1917-1918**—Maine builds ships that help win World War I.

**1941-1945**—Maine's factories provide shoes and uniforms for troops during World War II.

**1947**—A huge fire sweeps across Mount Desert Island, destroying buildings and 17,000 acres (6,800 hectares) of Acadia National Park.

**1954**—Maine starts a state income tax on individuals and companies.

**1972**—The Maine Yankee Atomic Power Plant begins operating.

**1980**—The United States government agrees to pay the Passamaquoddy and Penobscot people $81.5 million for land illegally taken 200 years ago.

**1992**—L. L. Bean celebrates its 80th anniversary as a store and catalog service of outdoor wear.

**1997**—Mainer William Cohen becomes Secretary of Defense under President Bill Clinton.

# Famous Mainers

**L. L. Bean** (1873-1967) Founder of the L. L. Bean factory, store, and catalog for outdoor gear in Freeport; born near Bethel.

**Milton Bradley** (1836-1911) Founder of the Milton Bradley Company, which makes board games such as Candyland and Battleship; born in Vienna.

**Dorothea Dix** (1802-1887) Reformer for improved care of the mentally ill; born in Hampden.

**John Ford** (1895-1973) Movie director and Academy Award-winner for such movies as *The Grapes of Wrath* (1940); born in Cape Elizabeth.

**Stephen King** (1947- ) Author of *The Stand, Misery,* and others; many of his books have been made into movies; born in Portland and lives in Bangor.

**Linda Lavin** (1937- ) Actress who starred in the television show "Alice"; born in Portland.

**Edna St. Vincent Millay** (1892-1950) Pulitzer Prize-winning poet who used New England backgrounds in her writings; born in Rockland.

**Edmund Muskie** (1914-1996) Governor of Maine (1955-1959) and U.S. senator (1959-1980); born in Rumford.

**Edwin Arlington Robinson** (1869-1935) Poet who won the first Pulitzer Prize in poetry (1922) and two others (1925 and 1928); born in Head Tide.

**Nelson Rockefeller** (1908-1979) Vice president of the United States (1974-1977); born in Bar Harbor.

**Joan Benoit Samuelson** (1957- ) Gold medalist in the 1984 Summer Olympics for the first women's marathon; born in Portland.

**Margaret Chase Smith** (1897-1995) First woman to serve both houses of Congress; born in Skowhegan.

**Samantha Smith** (1972-1985) Young girl who wrote to Yuri Andropov, the leader of the Soviet Union, in 1983 about world peace; Mount Samantha Smith was named for her; born in Houlton.

**Louis Sockalexis** (1871-1913) Professional baseball player with the Cleveland Spiders; the team was renamed the Cleveland Indians to honor him; born in Old Town.

**Francis Stanley** (1849-1918) and **Freelan Stanley** (1849-1940) Twin brothers who invented the Stanley Steamer automobile (1897); born in Kingfield.

**E. B. White** (1899-1985) Author of *Charlotte's Web* and other books; lived in Maine for 45 years.

# Words to Know

**Acadian**—a person of French descent who lived in early Nova Scotia

**clear-cutting**—cutting down whole areas of trees

**colony**—a group of people who settle in a different land but remain under the control of their native country

**environment**—the air, land, and water of a specific area

**fishing fleet**—a group of boats used for organized fishing

**glacier**—a huge sheet of slow-moving ice

**northeaster**—a strong windstorm that comes out of the northeast over the ocean

**prohibition**—the ban of the manufacture and sale of alcohol

**tidal shoreline**—land near islands, bays, and rivers that is touched by ocean waters

**upland**—land that is higher than surrounding land

**windjammer**—a large ship with two large sails that can move easily among other ships

# To Learn More

**Aylesworth, Thomas G. and Virginia L. Aylesworth**. *Northern New England*. New York: Chelsea House, 1991.

**Curtis, Wayne**. *Maine: Off the Beaten Path*. Old Saybrook, Conn.: The Globe Pequot Press, 1992.

**Engfer, LeeAnne**. *Maine*. Hello USA. Minneapolis: Lerner Publications, 1991.

**Fradin, Dennis B**. *Maine*. Sea to Shining Sea. Chicago: Children's Press, 1994.

You can read about the people, places, history, and everyday life in New England in *Yankee* magazine.

# Useful Addresses

**Acadia National Park**
P.O. Box 177
Bar Harbor, ME 04609

**Aroostook Farm**
Maine Agricultural Experiment Station
Houlton Road
Presque Isle, ME 04769

**Baxter State Park**
64 Balsam Drive
Millinocket, ME 04462

**Bethel Area Chamber of Commerce**
P.O. Box 439, Dept. M
Bethel, ME 04217

**Maine Maritime Museum & Shipyard**
243 Washington Street
Bath, ME 04530

**Museum of Portland Head Light**
1000 Shore Road
Cape Elizabeth, ME 04107

**Norlands Living History Center**
RR 2
Livermore Falls, ME 04254

# Internet Sites

**City.Net Maine**
http://www.city.net/countries/united_states/maine

**Travel.org—Maine**
http://travel.org/maine.html

**Maine State Government**
http://www.state.me.us

**Portland Head Light**
http://www.portlandheadlight.com

# Index